ENTREPRENEURIAL OPPORTUNITIES FOR BLACK WOMEN

A Guide to Starting Your Own Business

Ebony Precious

Copyright (c) 2023, Ebony Precious

All rights reserved. No part of this book may be reproduced, stored in a retrieval system, or transmitted in any form or by any means, electronic, mechanical, photocopying, recording, or otherwise, without the prior written permission of the copyright owner.

This book is sold subject to the condition that it shall not, by way of trade or otherwise, be lent, re-sold, hired out, or otherwise circulated without the publisher's prior consent in any form of binding or cover other than that in which it is published and without a similar condition including this condition being imposed on the subsequent purchaser.

This book is intended for general informational purposes only and is not intended to be a substitute for professional medical, legal, or financial advice. The author and the publisher shall not be held liable for any errors or omissions or any actions taken based on the information contained in this book.

TABLE OF CONTENTS

INTRODUCTION 4
   Definition of Entrepreneurship 5
   Importance of Entrepreneurial Opportunities for Black Women 7

UNDERSTANDING THE ENTREPRENEURIAL ENVIRONMENT 9
   Trends and Opportunities in the Market 10
   Black Women Entrepreneurs' Obstacles and Challenges 12

MAKING A BUSINESS PLAN 15
   Defining Your Business Idea 17
   Researching the Market 19
   Developing a Financial Plan 21

OBTAINING FUNDING AND ASSISTANCE 25
   Traditional Loan Alternatives 27
   Black Women Entrepreneur Grants 29
   Women-Owned Business Incubators and Accelerators 30

DEVELOP YOUR NETWORK AND BRAND 33
   Enhancing Your Personal Brand 35

SALES AND MARKETING 38
   Making a Marketing Strategy 40
   Effective Sales Strategies 43

LEGAL AND REGULATORY CONSIDERATIONS 47
   Business Formation and Organization 49
   Trademark and Intellectual Property Protection 51

All local, state, and federal laws must be followed 54
CONCLUSION 57
Support for Black Women Entrepreneurs 58

INTRODUCTION

Entrepreneurship is a powerful tool for creating economic opportunities and wealth for individuals and communities. Entrepreneurship can help Black women build a career and financial independence. This guide examines the unique challenges and opportunities that Black women face when starting a business and offers advice and strategies for success. This guide will help Black women entrepreneurs get started on their entrepreneurial journey, from finding the right business idea to managing finances to networking and marketing.

This guide is intended to provide an overview of the steps involved in becoming an entrepreneur and to empower Black women to take the first steps toward starting their own businesses. Black women entrepreneurs with the right mindset, resources, and knowledge can pursue their dreams and build successful businesses.

By the end of this guide, readers should be confident in their ability to start and run a successful business. They will learn how to develop a business idea, write a business plan, manage finances, and market the business to potential customers. Readers will also learn about the resources available to them to help them succeed as entrepreneurs.

By becoming an entrepreneur, Black women can gain financial independence and create a future of economic opportunity for themselves and their communities. This guide will provide the steps and knowledge needed to help Black women entrepreneurs achieve their goals.

Let's get started!

Definition of Entrepreneurship

Entrepreneurship is the process of starting a business or other venture and taking financial risks in order to reap potential rewards. It entails starting a new business or expanding an existing one, taking risks, and persevering. It is a major driver of economic growth and job creation.

Black women can benefit from entrepreneurship by starting their own businesses, which can lead to increased economic opportunities and job creation. Black women who own their own businesses can work their own hours, set their own pay rates, and create their own working environment. This autonomy can assist black women in achieving financial stability and independence. Furthermore, owning their own businesses can help black women build their own networks and increase their visibility within their industries.

Entrepreneurship can also provide black women with the opportunity to create jobs for others in their communities. This can lead to increased economic development and wealth creation in these communities. Furthermore, entrepreneurship can lead to increased economic power and influence for black women, which can help to break down barriers and create more opportunities for other black women.

Importance of Entrepreneurial Opportunities for Black Women

The significance of entrepreneurial opportunities for Black women cannot be overstated. For far too long, Black women have been denied the same educational and career opportunities as their white counterparts. As a result, there are fewer Black women in positions of power and influence, creating a cycle of poverty and inequality.

By starting their own businesses, Black women can break the cycle of poverty and inequality. Starting a business allows Black women to gain independence, financial stability, and control over their own destinies. With their own businesses, Black women can hire and empower other Black women, thereby creating job opportunities and economic growth in their communities.

Black women entrepreneurs can also use their businesses to address social issues and advocate for social change. Black women can use their businesses to challenge the status quo and promote positive change in their communities by providing a platform from which to speak out.

Furthermore, entrepreneurship provides Black women with the opportunity to gain visibility and recognition for their accomplishments. By showcasing their successes, Black women can become role models for other Black women, inspiring them to pursue their dreams and empowering them to pursue their entrepreneurial ambitions.

UNDERSTANDING THE ENTREPRENEURIAL ENVIRONMENT

Black women should begin by researching and studying successful entrepreneurs in their fields of interest in order to understand the entrepreneurial landscape. They should also investigate local resources and organizations that provide mentorship and guidance to entrepreneurs, as well as support networks that provide capital, resources, and other forms of assistance. Black women should also take advantage of online and in-person educational opportunities such as workshops, seminars, and conferences that provide insights into the entrepreneurial landscape. Finally, they should network with other entrepreneurs, both within and outside of their industry, to gain a better understanding of the challenges and opportunities that come with running a business.

Black women can gain a better understanding of the entrepreneurial landscape by doing the necessary research, attending relevant events, and networking with other entrepreneurs. They can make more informed decisions about pursuing entrepreneurship and better prepare for the challenges and opportunities that come with it with this knowledge.

Trends and Opportunities in the Market

Market trends and opportunities can be a very powerful tool for black women looking to grow and develop their businesses. With access to the most recent market data, black women can identify and capitalize on emerging opportunities. They can also use this information to identify potential growth areas and decide on the best course of action.

The ability to identify successful strategies and trends that are unique to the black community is one of the most important aspects of market trends and opportunities. Black women can develop unique approaches that are tailored to the needs of their target market by understanding the specific needs of the black community and the products and services that are most likely to be successful there. This will allow them to better serve their customers and expand their market share.

Furthermore, market trends and opportunities can be used to identify potential new revenue sources and expand existing businesses. By staying current on trends, black women can identify new opportunities and develop new products or services to meet the needs of their customers. This can help them increase their revenue and grow their businesses.

Finally, for a black woman reading this book, understanding market trends and opportunities can be a great way to gain a better understanding of the current market and what is possible. They can make better decisions and position their businesses for success if they understand the trends and opportunities in their market.

Black women can stay ahead of the competition and better position their businesses for success by capitalizing on market trends and opportunities.

Black Women Entrepreneurs' Obstacles and Challenges

Black women entrepreneurs face a unique set of challenges and barriers that other entrepreneurs do not. These challenges include a lack of capital, insufficient networks, a lack of resources, and cultural and gender biases.

1. **Inadequate Capital Access:** Black women entrepreneurs are frequently unable to obtain traditional sources of capital, such as venture capital or angel investors. They may have difficulty obtaining bank loans, which can be a major impediment to starting and growing a business.

2. **Inadequate Networks:** Because black women entreprencurs may not have access to the same networks as other entrepreneurs, finding mentors and potential customers may be more difficult.

3. Inadequate Access to Resources: Black women entrepreneurs frequently face difficulties in obtaining the resources they require to start and grow their businesses. Access to technology, education, and professional networks are examples of these.

4. Cultural and Gender Bias: Black women entrepreneurs may face challenges in the business world due to cultural and gender biases. They may be passed over for opportunities and receive less support than their peers.

5. Inadequate Technical Knowledge: Many black women entrepreneurs may struggle to develop the technical skills required to start and grow their businesses, such as marketing, finance, and business strategy.

6. Balancing Work and Family Responsibilities: Many black women entrepreneurs struggle to balance the demands of starting and growing a business with their domestic responsibilities, such as caring for children and elderly relatives.

7. Underrepresentation: Black women entrepreneurs are frequently underrepresented in the entrepreneurial community and in the media, limiting their visibility and access to opportunities.

Despite these challenges and barriers, an increasing number of black female entrepreneurs are overcoming them and succeeding in business. Black women entrepreneurs can continue to make strides in the business world with the help of their communities, the government, and private organizations.

MAKING A BUSINESS PLAN

Regardless of the industry, developing a business plan is a critical step in starting a business. A business plan can be a valuable tool for evaluating the potential success of a black woman's venture, as well as a roadmap for setting and achieving goals.

An executive summary, which is a brief overview of the business, including its purpose and goals; a description of the business, including its products and services; a market analysis, which identifies target customers and their needs; a competitive analysis, which looks at the competition and how the business will differentiate itself from them; financial projections, which project the business's expected profits and losses; and a management plan should all be included in a business plan.

The executive summary should also include a mission statement that expresses the business's purpose and core values; a vision statement that outlines the company's long-term goals; and a SWOT analysis that outlines the company's strengths and weaknesses, as well as the opportunities and threats it may face.

A business plan should include, in addition to the executive summary, a marketing plan that outlines strategies for reaching and engaging customers; an operations plan that details how the business will operate on a day-to-day basis; and a financial plan that outlines the capital required to start the business and the sources of funding.

The business plan for black women starting a business should also include a discussion of how their unique experiences as black women will be leveraged. For example, they may be able to draw on their own experiences as well as those of other black women in the industry to develop an innovative business approach and connect with potential customers.

Finally, a business plan should include a timeline for achieving the company's goals, as well as a plan for dealing with unexpected problems. A well-written business plan can be a valuable tool for black women starting a business, assisting them in evaluating their venture's potential success and planning for the future.

Black women can set themselves up for success as they embark on their entrepreneurial journey by developing a comprehensive business plan.

Defining Your Business Idea

Defining your business idea is the process of determining the purpose and scope of your company, as well as the products or services you intend to provide. It is an important step in the process of starting a business because it allows you to determine your company's mission and goals.

Defining a business idea can be a way for black women to gain economic opportunity and independence. Black women can become entrepreneurs with the right business idea and plans, providing economic stability and security for themselves and their families. This can also be a means of increasing wealth in the black community because black-owned businesses can provide jobs and resources to other black people.

When considering a business venture, black women must consider their unique strengths, experiences, and perspectives. This can assist them in identifying an idea that aligns with their interests and skill sets and has a positive impact on the black community.

It is also critical to consider the market and the potential customers you are attempting to reach. Researching trends, identifying customer needs, and researching potential competitors can assist you in developing a viable, profitable, and impactful business idea.

Finally, it is critical to developing a business plan that details your objectives, strategies, and financial projections. This plan can assist you in determining the viability of your idea and obtaining financing to launch your business.

Black women can create economic opportunity and security for themselves and their families while also positively impacting the black community by taking the time to define a business idea.

Researching the Market

Market research is essential for any business owner, but it is especially important for black women entrepreneurs. Market research assists entrepreneurs in developing a better understanding of their target customers, the competitive landscape, and industry trends that will affect their business. By conducting this research, black female entrepreneurs will be able to develop effective marketing strategies, create products and services that meet the needs of their customers, and identify the most profitable business opportunities.

When conducting market research, black women entrepreneurs should concentrate on understanding their target customers' needs, wants, and values. This entails investigating the demographics of the target market as well as the types of products and services they require. Furthermore, black women entrepreneurs should gather information about their competitors, such as the types of products and services they offer, pricing strategies, and marketing tactics. This will assist entrepreneurs in identifying areas where they can distinguish themselves and gain a competitive advantage.

Identifying industry trends is another critical step in market research. This entails researching the most recent industry developments, such as new technologies, regulations, or customer preferences. Black women entrepreneurs can stay ahead of the competition and capitalize on potential business opportunities by understanding these trends.

Finally, black women entrepreneurs should evaluate their company's potential profitability. This entails investigating the costs of starting and running a business, as well as the potential revenue generated. Black women entrepreneurs can make informed decisions about their business strategy by understanding the potential profits.

By conducting thorough market research, black women entrepreneurs can gain valuable insights that will assist them in making informed business decisions. Black women entrepreneurs can develop effective strategies, create products and services that meet the needs of their target customers and identify the most profitable business opportunities with the right market research.

It is also critical for black women entrepreneurs to keep in mind that market research is a continuous process. As the industry and customer preferences shift, black women entrepreneurs should conduct ongoing research to stay current on the latest trends and opportunities. This will assist them in staying ahead of the competition and building a successful business.

Developing a Financial Plan

When a black woman wants to start a business, she must develop a financial plan to ensure the venture's success. A financial plan will assist her in determining how much money she will need to start the business, the sources of funds available to her, and how she will manage her finances once the business is operational.

The first step in developing a financial plan is calculating the startup costs. This includes the cost of registering the business, purchasing supplies, hiring employees, and any other expenses related to the business's launch. She should also consider alternative sources of income, such as loans, grants, and investments.

After determining the startup costs, she should develop a budget that includes all of the expenses associated with running the business, such as payroll, taxes, rent, and other operational costs. This budget should also include a strategy for how she will use her income to cover these expenses while also saving for the future.

The following step is to consider how she will obtain capital to fund the business. She should investigate various financing options, such as obtaining business loans, establishing lines of credit, or obtaining venture capital. She should also think about the various types of grants and other funding options available to minority-owned businesses.

Finally, she should devise a strategy for managing her finances once the business is up and running. This includes keeping track of income and expenses, putting money aside for taxes, saving for retirement, and planning for business expansion.

A black woman can ensure the success of her business venture by developing a financial plan. She can ensure that her business is well-funded, well-managed, and profitable with careful planning and research.

It is important to note that a black woman should consider other factors when starting a business, such as the legal structure of the business, the type of insurance she requires, and the local regulations she must follow. A black woman can ensure that she has created a comprehensive financial plan that will help her succeed in her business venture by researching these topics.

A black woman can start her business on the right foot and ensure its success by developing a financial plan. She can ensure that her business is properly funded and managed and that she can meet her objectives, with careful planning and research.

OBTAINING FUNDING AND ASSISTANCE

Starting a business, especially for Black women, can be a daunting task. Not only do they face the same challenges as other entrepreneurs, but they also face systemic racism, sexism, and other forms of discrimination, which can make it even more difficult to obtain the funding and support they require to succeed.

Fortunately, Black women who want to start a business can access a variety of resources. To get you started, here are a few pointers:

1. Expand Your Network: Making connections with people who understand the unique challenges that Black women face when starting a business can be extremely beneficial. Reach out to people in your neighborhood, join professional organizations, and attend events geared specifically toward Black entrepreneurs. This will assist you in locating potential investors, mentors, and collaborators who are interested in your success.

2. Take Advantage of Government Programs: The federal government, as well as local and state governments, offer programs and resources to assist entrepreneurs from all walks of life. Investigate the available resources and apply for those that are relevant to your company.

3. Look for Grants: There are several organizations that offer grants to Black women entrepreneurs. Look for organizations that have goals similar to yours and apply for grants from them.

4. Use Crowdfunding: Crowdfunding is an excellent way to raise funds for your business without relying on traditional investors. Plum Alley and Backstage Capital are two crowdfunding platforms that specialize in assisting Black women entrepreneurs.

5. Think about Small Business Loans: Small business loans can provide the capital you need to get your business started. Consider both government-backed loans and private lenders who specialize in lending to minority-owned businesses.

Black women entrepreneurs can find the funding and support they need to start and grow their businesses by taking advantage of the resources available. Anything is possible with the right resources and support.

Traditional Loan Alternatives

A black woman looking to start a business has several traditional loan options. To begin, she will need to develop a business plan that outlines her company's goals, objectives, and strategies. This plan should include a market analysis, a financial plan, and an estimated budget. After she has completed the business plan, she can begin researching traditional loan options by visiting her local bank or credit union.

Typical loan options include applying for a small business loan or a line of credit. To apply for a loan, the black woman must submit her credit history, business plan, and financial statements to the lender. It is important to note that loan requirements and interest rates may vary depending on loan size, loan length, and business type.

The black woman should also think about applying for grants or awards designed specifically for minority entrepreneurs. The Office of Women's Business Ownership (OWBO) of the U.S. Small Business Administration (SBA) provides grants to black women entrepreneurs. A quick internet search can also help her find other grant opportunities.

Traditional loan options can be a great way for a black woman who wants to start a business to get the funding she needs to get started. To increase her chances of success, she should research loan options and develop a detailed business plan.

Finally, it is critical for black women entrepreneurs to seek support from their local community. There are numerous resources available to help black women entrepreneurs succeed, ranging from networking events to mentorship programs. A black woman entrepreneur can make her business dreams a reality by utilizing these resources.

Black Women Entrepreneur Grants

Grants for Black Women Entrepreneurs are special grants available to women who identify as Black and want to start or expand a business. These grants are intended to provide financial assistance and resources to Black women entrepreneurs in order to help them succeed in their business ventures.

There are a variety of grants available specifically to Black women entrepreneurs. These grants can be used to help with startup costs such as purchasing equipment and supplies, marketing materials, and legal fees. Grants can also be used to fund research and development or to provide mentorship or access to business resources.

Grants can help Black female entrepreneurs gain access to capital that would otherwise be difficult to obtain, such as venture capital or bank loans.

They can also give entrepreneurs access to resources that will help them succeed, such as networking opportunities, workshops, and training.

In addition to grants, Black women entrepreneurs can access other resources such as business incubators, accelerators, and crowdfunding platforms. These resources can connect entrepreneurs with mentors, startup capital, and other resources that can help them succeed.

Women-Owned Business Incubators and Accelerators

Women-owned business incubators and accelerators are organizations that assist female entrepreneurs in starting, developing, and growing their businesses. These organizations provide resources and networks, as well as mentoring and coaching, educational programming, and capital. They also provide a supportive environment in which women are encouraged to take risks and pursue their dreams.

These organizations' mission is to empower female entrepreneurs to reach their full potential and leave a lasting impact on their communities. These organizations can assist women in becoming more successful business owners and entrepreneurs by providing access to resources and networks.

These organizations' assistance can range from providing access to capital to mentoring to developing a business plan. Many incubators and accelerators will also offer educational programs, such as workshops and seminars, to assist women in understanding the business landscape and making sound decisions.

In addition to resources and networks, incubators and accelerators for women-owned businesses can offer networking opportunities and connections to potential investors. These organizations can assist women in obtaining the funding they require to grow their businesses by connecting them with potential investors.

Finally, women-owned business incubators and accelerators can provide a platform for female entrepreneurs to showcase their businesses and products. Hosting events such as pitch competitions, conferences, and exhibitions is one example.

Access to resources and networks, mentoring and coaching educational programming, and capital, incubators, and accelerators for women-owned businesses are all critical to assisting female entrepreneurs in reaching their full potential and making a positive difference in their communities.

These organizations contribute to a more diverse and inclusive business landscape that is better equipped to support female entrepreneurs by providing access to resources and networks. This has the potential to result in more diverse and successful businesses, as well as a more equitable economy.

DEVELOP YOUR NETWORK AND BRAND

Building a network and brand as a black woman entrepreneur can be difficult, but it is possible to succeed with the right approach and resources. Here are some steps that may be useful:

Define your brand by doing the following: Begin by defining your company's mission, the products or services it provides, and what distinguishes it from competitors. This will assist you in developing a distinct brand identity and positioning yourself in the market.

Create a professional network: Networking is essential for any business, but it is especially important for black women entrepreneurs. Joining local business organizations, attending events, and connecting with other business owners online are all options.

Make use of social media: Social media is an effective tool for increasing brand awareness and reaching new customers. Choose platforms where your target audience is active and establish a strong presence by posting engaging content on a regular basis.

Seek mentorship: Find a mentor who can guide and support you as you grow your business. This can be a business owner in your field, a successful entrepreneur, or a professional with relevant expertise.

Attend conferences and workshops to learn about the latest trends in your industry and to network with other business owners. These events are also excellent places to network and gain brand exposure.

Collaboration with other businesses can help you expand your reach and build relationships with potential customers and partners. Consider collaborating with complementary businesses to provide shared products or services.

Building strong, authentic relationships is essential for developing a successful network and brand. Spend time getting to know your customers and partners, and treat them with respect and honesty.

Maintain your values and stay true to your brand: Building a successful business requires you to maintain your values and stay true to your brand. Be true to yourself and always strive to do the right thing, even if it means making difficult decisions.

Building a network and brand takes time and effort, but success as a black woman entrepreneur is possible with dedication and perseverance.

Enhancing Your Personal Brand

Building a personal brand is critical for any woman, especially a black woman, looking to start a business. Personal branding is an important part of promoting yourself and your business, so make sure that it is strong and reflects your values and goals.

Here are some pointers to assist a black woman in developing her personal brand:

1. Determine Your Values: It is critical to determine your values and then use them to guide your decisions. Understanding your core values will help you ensure that your personal brand is consistent with these values. Knowing your values will also make communicating them to others easier.

2. Create an Online Presence: It is critical to creating an online presence in order to promote your personal brand. Having a website, blog, or social media account is an example of this. Make sure that the content you post reflects your values and goals.

3. Network: Networking is an essential component of developing your personal brand. Attend events and meet ups, and connect with others in your industry on social media.

4. Be Consistent: When it comes to personal branding, consistency is essential. Maintain a consistent message across all platforms by posting on a regular basis.

5. Tell Your Story: Telling your story is an essential part of personal branding. Share your stories and use them to connect with others.

A black woman can effectively build her personal brand and promote her business by following these tips. It is critical to remember that personal branding is a long-term process, so you must be consistent in your efforts. You will be able to build a strong and successful personal brand with dedication and hard work.

SALES AND MARKETING

To ensure success, black women who want to start a business should focus on effective marketing and sales strategies. Creating a comprehensive marketing plan is critical for any business, but especially for black women-owned businesses. An effective marketing strategy will combine traditional and digital marketing tactics.

Print media such as newspapers, magazines, and flyers are examples of traditional marketing strategies. These can be used to raise brand awareness and reach out to local customers. Furthermore, these traditional strategies can be used to reach out to and build relationships with potential customers in the larger community.

Social media platforms such as Facebook, Twitter, and Instagram are used in digital marketing strategies to reach out to potential customers and build relationships. This can be accomplished by creating content, engaging with customers, and running targeted advertisements. Furthermore, social media makes it simple to track customer interactions and feedback. This can help businesses better understand what their customers want and how to reach them.

Black women-owned businesses must also employ effective sales strategies. Creating a sales pitch and understanding the needs of the customer are critical for any business. Discounts, loyalty programs, and free samples can also help to attract and retain customers. Understanding the needs of the customer and providing excellent customer service is also essential for any business.

Finally, it is critical for black women-owned businesses to network with other businesses in the community. Attending networking events and connecting with other entrepreneurs can help with this. Partnerships with other businesses can also be formed to create unique products and services.

Finally, effective marketing and sales strategies are critical for any business, particularly black women-owned businesses. Using a combination of traditional and digital marketing strategies, developing a sales pitch, and establishing relationships with other businesses can all contribute to success. Businesses can build a loyal customer base and ensure long-term success by understanding their customers' needs and providing excellent customer service.

Making a Marketing Strategy

Creating a marketing plan is critical for any business, but especially for Black female entrepreneurs, who are frequently underrepresented in the business world. A marketing plan lays out the strategies and tactics that will be used to reach a specific target audience, as well as the budget and timeline for those efforts. Black women entrepreneurs should start by understanding their target audience and defining their unique value proposition in order to create a successful marketing plan.

The first step in developing a marketing strategy is identifying the target audience. A thorough understanding of the target audience will assist the business owner in determining the most effective marketing channels and tactics. When choosing marketing channels, black women entrepreneurs should consider their target audience's demographics, interests, and needs. They should also pay close attention to the preferences of their target audience for digital, print, and social media platforms.

The second step is to develop a distinct value proposition. A unique value proposition is a statement that clearly articulates the advantages of a company's product or services. It should be tailored to the intended audience and memorable enough to catch their attention. In addition to the unique value proposition, black women entrepreneurs should develop a tagline or slogan. This will help the company stand out and leave an impression on potential customers.

The final step is to create a budget. Entrepreneurs should decide how much money they are willing to spend on each marketing channel. A budget should include costs for content creation, customer engagement, and advertising. Black female entrepreneurs should also consider hiring outside help to manage their marketing efforts.

Finally, Black women entrepreneurs should develop a marketing timeline. This timeline should include specific deadlines for when content should be created, campaigns launched and results measured. It should also include the milestones and goals that the business owner hopes to achieve.

For Black women entrepreneurs who want to reach their target audience and build a successful business, developing a marketing plan is essential. Black women entrepreneurs can create a comprehensive, effective marketing plan by understanding their target audience, defining a unique value proposition, developing a budget, and creating a timeline.

Effective Sales Strategies

Starting a business can be a rewarding and challenging experience for anyone, but for Black women, the journey can present unique challenges. Nonetheless, Black women entrepreneurs can achieve success in the business world with careful planning and effective sales strategies.

Here are some effective sales strategies for Black women starting a business:

1. Create a Solid Business Plan: Creating a solid business plan is the first step for Black women who want to start a business. A detailed description of the business, its goals, the strategies required to achieve these goals, and a financial outlook should all be included in a business plan. This plan is critical for pitching potential investors and obtaining funding. A business plan should also be reviewed on a regular basis to ensure that it is still relevant in today's business environment.

2. Take Advantage of Networking Opportunities: Networking is a valuable resource for Black women entrepreneurs. It aids in the development of relationships, the identification of business opportunities, and the formation of strategic alliances. Attending conferences, networking events, and other professional gatherings can help you make business contacts. 3. Invest in Quality Marketing Strategies: Investing in quality marketing strategies is essential for an effective sales process. Investing in digital marketing initiatives such as content marketing, search engine optimization, and social media marketing should be considered by black women entrepreneurs. Traditional marketing tactics such as direct mail, print advertising, and radio and television commercials can also be effective in raising awareness and engagement.

4. Make Use of Strategic Partnerships: Strategic partnerships can help you expand your customer reach, generate more leads, and increase your sales. Black women entrepreneurs should actively seek out partnerships with other businesses, organizations, and individuals who can assist them in growing their businesses.

5. Use Sales Technology: Investing in sales technology can significantly improve sales process efficiency. To streamline the sales process and maximize customer engagement, black women entrepreneurs should use tools such as customer relationship management (CRM) software, sales analytics, and lead generation tools.

6. Make Customer Experience a Priority: Providing an excellent customer experience is critical for effective sales. In order to foster loyalty and increase sales, black women entrepreneurs should prioritize customer service, product quality, and customer satisfaction. They should also consider offering incentives such as discounts, coupons, and loyalty programs to keep customers engaged and returning.

7. Establish SMART Goals: SMART goals (specific, measurable, achievable, relevant, and time-bound) are essential for effectively managing the sales process.

Black women entrepreneurs should set realistic and attainable goals and devise a plan to achieve them. In order to achieve these objectives, they should also track progress and adjust their strategies as needed.

Black women entrepreneurs can increase their chances of success and maximize their sales potential by developing a business plan, utilizing networking opportunities, investing in quality marketing strategies, utilizing strategic partnerships, utilizing sales technology, prioritizing customer experience, and setting SMART goals.

LEGAL AND REGULATORY CONSIDERATIONS

It is critical for black women to understand the legal and regulatory considerations that come with starting a business. These considerations are critical to ensuring the business's successful launch and operation.

The first step in the legal and regulatory considerations process is to research and comprehend the relevant laws and regulations in the state and/or locality where the business will be operated. This includes investigating tax laws, licensing requirements, and any other laws or regulations that may have an impact on the business. It is also critical to be aware of the local and state regulations that apply to the type of business being launched. A restaurant, for example, must be aware of zoning and health regulations, whereas a retail business must be aware of consumer protection laws.

After understanding the applicable laws and regulations, the next step is to register the business and obtain the necessary licenses and permits. This may include a business license, a sales tax permit, and/or a zoning permit, depending on the type of business. It is also critical that any employees be registered with the appropriate state and/or federal agencies, such as the Internal Revenue Service (IRS).

The following step in the legal and regulatory considerations process is to think about any contracts that may be required. Contracts with vendors, customers, and any other parties involved in the business are included. It is critical that these contracts are written in a clear and concise manner and are legally binding.

Finally, black women should think about any insurance policies that might be required for the business. This includes liability insurance to protect the company from potential lawsuits, property insurance to protect the company's physical assets, and any other types of insurance that may be necessary.

Black women can ensure that their businesses are properly set up and in compliance with all applicable laws and regulations by understanding the legal and regulatory considerations associated with starting a business. This will help to ensure that the company is successful and can continue to operate for many years.

Business Formation and Organization

As a black woman, starting a business can be an empowering and rewarding experience. However, many important steps must be taken prior to launching a business, and understanding the business formation and structure is critical to success.

The first step in starting a business is determining the type of business you want to start. Sole proprietorship, partnership, limited liability company (LLC), and corporation are all examples of business structures. Each structure provides varying degrees of liability protection and taxation. It is critical to research and comprehends each type of business formation and structure before deciding on the best option for your company.

After deciding on a business structure, the next step is to register the company with the local, state, and federal governments. This may entail submitting the necessary paperwork and legal documents, such as the Articles of Incorporation or LLC Operating Agreement. To ensure that the business is properly registered, it is critical to consult with an attorney and/or an accountant.

Following the registration of the company, the next step is to obtain all necessary licenses and permits. This may entail obtaining a business license, a tax identification number, and any required permits. Because this can be a time-consuming process, it is critical to research the requirements for each specific license or permit and begin the process as soon as possible.

The final step is to secure the funding required to launch the business. This may entail applying for loans, grants, or other types of funding. It is also critical to manage the business's finances and create a budget to ensure the company's financial stability.

Trademark and Intellectual Property Protection

Black women who want to start a business should understand the value of the intellectual property (IP) and trademark protection. Intellectual property (IP) is a legal term for intangible assets such as ideas, brand names, designs, logos, and slogans. It is critical to protect intellectual property because it allows a company to protect its creative works, ensure brand identity, and prevent competitors from infringing on their rights.

Trademark protection is an important component of intellectual property protection. A trademark is a distinguishing sign, design, or expression that distinguishes one source's product or service from those of competitors. Businesses should register their trademarks to protect their brand and prevent competitors from using their name or logo.

When a black woman starts a business, she must be aware of the steps she must take to protect her intellectual property and trademark. She should investigate the trademark laws in the jurisdiction where she is doing business, as well as the requirements in other countries where she may want to expand. She should also conduct research on her competitors to ensure that her company name and logo do not infringe on their rights.

After she has completed her research, she will register her trademark. In the United States, this can be accomplished by submitting a trademark application to the US Patent and Trademark Office (USPTO). If she wants to expand globally, she should consider registering her trademark in other countries.

Once her trademark has been registered, the black woman must monitor it and enforce her rights. This means she should keep an eye out for any other companies that may be using her name or logo without her permission. If she discovers any such cases, she should take appropriate action to protect her rights.

A black woman should consider other ways to protect her intellectual property in addition to registering and monitoring her trademark. This includes obtaining copyright, patents, and trade secrets, as well as taking precautions to safeguard her confidential information.

Black women who want to start their own businesses should understand the value of the intellectual property and trademark protection. They can ensure that their brand identity is protected from competitors and that their creative works are not infringed upon by taking the necessary steps to protect their IP.

IP and trademark protection are critical for all businesses, but especially for black women who want to start their own. They can protect their business and maintain their brand identity by taking the necessary steps to protect their intellectual property.

All local, state, and federal laws must be followed

Starting a business can be a difficult and daunting task for any woman, but for Black women, the additional challenges can be even more difficult. Compliance with local, state, and federal regulations is just one of many challenges that must be overcome before a business can be launched. Understanding the regulations and laws that must be followed in order to remain compliant is critical for any business owner, but it can be especially difficult for Black women who may lack the same resources or knowledge as their white counterparts.

Understanding which regulations apply to your business is the first step in ensuring compliance with local, state, and federal regulations. This can be a challenging task because regulations vary greatly depending on the type of business and location. Furthermore, business owners must stay current on any changes or updates that may occur during the life of their company.

Black women should seek assistance from the Small Business Administration (SBA) to ensure compliance with local, state, and federal regulations. The SBA provides a number of resources and services to assist business owners in understanding, complying with, and managing their regulations. Furthermore, the SBA provides access to Small Business Development Centers, which can assist entrepreneurs in developing and implementing effective business plans and strategies.

Once a company is up and running, Black women should contact their local chamber of commerce. Chambers of commerce can provide invaluable resources to business owners, such as networking opportunities and compliance resources. Furthermore, many chambers of commerce offer workshops and seminars to assist business owners in understanding the regulations and laws that apply to them.

Finally, Black women should think about joining local and national trade organizations and associations. Trade associations and organizations can connect you to a variety of resources, such as educational materials and legal advice. Furthermore, many of these organizations offer mentorship opportunities and host events that can assist business owners in staying current on legal and regulatory changes.

CONCLUSION

For Black women, starting a business can be a rewarding and empowering experience, and there are numerous opportunities for entrepreneurship in today's economy. Black women can achieve success and build thriving businesses by understanding the unique challenges and barriers that Black women face as entrepreneurs and by seeking resources and support from organizations and networks. Whether you're a seasoned entrepreneur or just getting started, the guide to starting your own business contains useful information and advice to help you turn your vision into a reality. Black women can create their own entrepreneurial opportunities and have a positive impact on their communities and the world with hard work, dedication, and a willingness to take risks.

We hope this guide has been useful in providing insight into the many potential entrepreneurial opportunities for black women. You can become a successful entrepreneur and build an innovative and profitable business with dedication, commitment, and the right resources. Best wishes on your entrepreneurial endeavors!

Support for Black Women Entrepreneurs

Black female entrepreneurs face unique obstacles, such as systemic barriers and a lack of resources. Despite these challenges, black women are launching successful businesses and transforming the face of entrepreneurship. We want to encourage these women to keep moving forward. Your dedication and perseverance are inspiring, and your contributions to the business world are priceless. Remember to celebrate your accomplishments, no matter how minor they appear. Also, never underestimate the value of self-care and taking time for yourself.

You are not on your own. There are numerous organizations and networks dedicated to empowering black women entrepreneurs. Seek mentorship, advice, and support from these organizations. And don't be afraid to form your own collaborations and partnerships. When we work together, we make the business world a better place.

Trust yourself and your ideas. Your distinct viewpoint and experiences add value to the table, and your ideas have the potential to make a significant difference. Allow no one to tell you that your ideas aren't good enough or that you're not cut out for entrepreneurship. Follow your interests and have faith in your abilities.

Continue to be strong. Entrepreneurship is not easy, and there will be bumps in the road. However, it is critical to stay focused on your objectives and to keep moving forward. Remember why you started, and understand that every obstacle is an opportunity to grow and learn.

You are trailblazers, risk takers, and game changers, black women entrepreneurs. Continue to shine, and know that you have so many people rooting for you.

www.ingramcontent.com/pod-product-compliance
Lightning Source LLC
Chambersburg PA
CBHW050331220526

45465CB00018B/1915